Life in China

Liz Chung

INFOMAX COMMON CORE READERS

Rosen Classroom™

New York

Published in 2013 by The Rosen Publishing Group, Inc.
29 East 21st Street, New York, NY 10010

Book Design: Michael Harmon

Photo Credits: Cover Jakrit Jiraratwaro/Shutterstock.com; p. 4 Image Source/Image Source/Getty Images;
p. 5 © iStockphoto.com/Nikada; p. 6 © iStockphoto.com/rest; p. 7 © iStockphoto.com/bo1982; p. 8 Iain Masterton/
Photographer's Choice/Getty Images; p. 9 TonyV3112/Shutterstock.com; p. 10 (sun) Serg64/Shutterstock.com;
p. 10 (moon) worldwildlifewonders/Shutterstock.com; p. 10 (cat) dinadesign/Shutterstock.com; p. 10 (dog) Margarita
Borodina/Shutterstock.com; p. 11 tristan tan/Shutterstock.com; p. 12 Chiyacat/Shutterstock.com; p. 13 Fabio Sabatini/
Flickr Select/Getty Images; p. 14 Digital Vision/Photodisc/Getty Images; pp. 15, 16, 17 iStockphoto/Thinkstock.com; pp.
18, 20 Hemera/Thinkstock.com; p. 19 TonyRo Image Stock/Thinkstock.com; p. 21 Christian Kober/Robert Harding World
Imagery/Getty Images; p. 22 YANGCHAO/Shutterstock.com.

ISBN: 978-1-4488-9025-5
6-pack ISBN: 978-1-4488-9026-2

Manufactured in the United States of America

CPSIA Compliance Information: Batch #WS12RC: For further information contact Rosen Publishing, New York, New York at 1-800-237-9932.

Word Count: 340

Contents

Welcome to China

China is a country in Asia. It's far away from the United States. It's a lot different from our country.

A lot of people live in China. China has more people than any other country. People from China are called Chinese.

China has different kinds of land. It has **mountains** and forests. China has one of the longest rivers in the world.

School is important in China. Children go to school six days a week!

Learning Languages

Chinese children learn different **languages** in school.

Some people in China speak **Mandarin**.

Mandarin is different from English. It uses tiny pictures instead of letters and words. The pictures stand for words or ideas.

Chinese Words

sun	太阳	
moon	月亮	
cat	猫	
dog	狗	

Important Symbols

Red is the most important color in China. Sometimes, it's a symbol. A symbol is something that stands for something else.

Red stands for good luck. China's flag is red.

It also has gold stars.

Chinese people use red paper to make **lanterns**.

They use them on important holidays. Red lanterns

stand for good luck.

People in China love dragons. The dragon is strong.

It's a symbol of luck, too. The dragon looks scary,

but it's not!

China also has a lucky plant. It's called **bamboo**.

Bamboo is tall and green. It grows like a tree.

Pandas eat bamboo. They live in the mountains.

People like pandas a lot. They're also a symbol

of China.

Rice and Tea

The Chinese people love to drink tea. They drink it hot or cold. Tea comes from parts of a plant.

China's food is different from our food. People in China eat a lot of rice. They eat it for breakfast, lunch, and dinner.

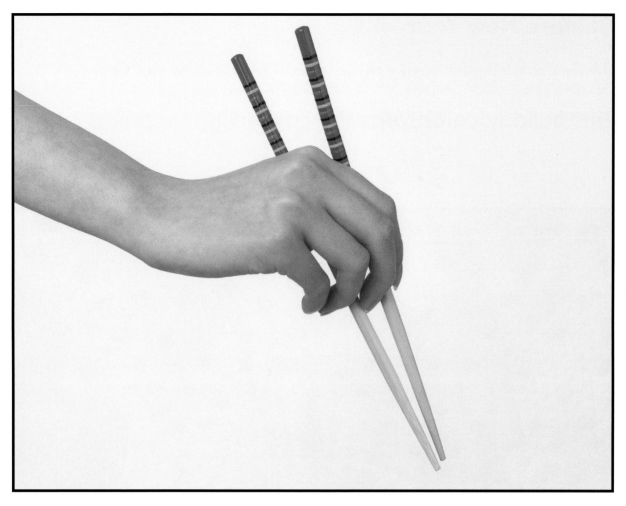

In China, people eat with chopsticks. Chopsticks are long and made out of wood. People need two chopsticks to eat.

Chinese New Year

China's biggest holiday is the Chinese New Year.

This holiday **celebrates** the beginning of spring.

People spend the Chinese New Year with their families. They wish for good luck and to be happy. This holiday is very fun.

There's a lot to learn about life in China. What do you know about China?

Glossary

bamboo (bam-BOO) A kind of grass that grows as tall as a tree.

celebrate (SEH-luh-brayt) To honor a holiday.

language (LAN-gwij) Words that people write or speak.

lantern (LAN-tuhrn) A covered light that can be carried.

Mandarin (MAN-duh-ruhn) A language spoken in China.

mountain (MAUHN-tuhn) A very tall hill made of rock.

Index